Small Stones
from the River

ALSO BY KAT LEHMANN

Moon Full of Moons

Small Stones
from the River

MEDITATIONS AND MICROPOEMS

Kat Lehmann

ISBN: 154555580X
ISBN-13: 978-1545555804

Cover Art by Subhashini Chandramani
https://neelavanam.in/
subhashini.chandramani@gmail.com

Published by 29 Trees Press
https://www.facebook.com/29Trees
29Trees@sbcglobal.net

Library of Congress Control Number: 2017909228
CreateSpace Independent Publishing Platform, North Charleston, SC

First Edition

10 9 8 7 6 5 4 3 2 1

DEDICATION

The unknown creates an opportunity for us to be hopeful and have faith. When we stretch into the unknown, we open ourselves to possibility. *Small Stones from the River* is dedicated to the those who walk journeys of becoming and, in doing so, solidify the hopefulness and faith around them.

In particular, I am grateful for the blessings of the following people:

to my family for their steadfast love and support, particularly KSVVNA and D&D

to Subha for her treasured friendship, visual artistry, and generous heart

to Tom for helping me leave a mark that sings

to Ken, Sol, Violet, Subha, McCall, Brian, Stephanie, and Dave for early readings

to other birds along the path: Anne, PL, Kim, Jill, Bruce, Dave

Love is a nutrient, a cofactor for growth.
Love is a gravity. We are made to come together.

ACKNOWLEDGMENTS

Grateful acknowledgment is made to the editors of the following literary journals, where some of the pieces in this collection first appeared.

Atlas Poetica (2015): (the time I thought)

hedgerow: a journal of small poems (2016): (dormant buds)

Moonbathing (2016): (fragments of an overactive mind)

Neverending Story / One Man's Maple Moon (2016): (each of them wants a part of me), with gratitude to the editor for translation of the poem

red lights (2016): (the music of falling apart)

The Bamboo Hut (2015): (the things I know without looking)

tinywords (2016): (if only happiness were easy)

PEOPLE TO WORDS

You might ask me to distill a truth
into a handful of words that somehow
transcend their meanings,
only you would not ask, really, and
it's not exactly truth,
but something like experience or urgency,
and there is so much of that these days,
with a possibility among the billions
that we will connect
or hope to cross a dangling kite-line with
the loose strand of another
to tangle for a moment.
Like birds flying over the highway, we are
living lives that seem to have nothing
to do with another,
yet as our paths cross on the perpendicular,
I recognize something in another being who
recognizes something in me.
We are travelers sharing the stream,
only the stream is experience,
and experience is words,
because people are not birds above the highway, and
the perspective isn't of one in-the-sky
and another one grounded, but
of two gravity-bound wanderers.
What kind of connection could nourish us like that
and what perspective could level us eye-to-eye,
bringing people to words for nourishment
until they untangle
and fly away.

pretend
I am handing these words
to you
written on a piece of paper
torn from a corner
you put them
in your pocket
for later

the mountain before you
is just a symbol

what you climb
step by step
is yourself

you cannot
reassemble
all the shards that litter your path

if that
was your assignment
you would never be done

sharing
is how we find each other
like birds finding birds
that sing
the same song

we tend to see
a person
in the moment
not
as the journey
they traveled to get here

see slowly
to see a bit more
the world
is always blooming
somewhere
in endless springtime

the small things make up everything there is

the seeds
of who I am
were always within me

how could it not be so?

the seeds
of who I will become
are already within me

how could it not be so?

the limitations
I place
on the dreams
of others
are the same limitations
I place
on myself

praise the flower
when it is no longer
blooming

all phases of the cycle are
necessary
to enable the flower
to become

each day
something withers
and
each day
something blooms

happiness
has a chance to grow
when we see
dandelions
as flowers

when we notice
the grandiose
within a small expression
of beauty

when we cherish
a stumble
as more of a reason
for love

I go beneath the layers of a day

I let the sweat drip

I walk in the rain

I adjust my mind
and find what is perfect
in its imperfection

in this way
I reclaim my energy

and optimize what is outside
from the inside

your legacy
is your love

that's the best thing you do

love's inclusivity
may be its most challenging
yet essential
feature

the realization
that you feel love
for someone
because
you are friends
with their beautiful imperfections

many someones

when you
burn the food
trip over your feet
trip over your free will
sometimes I feel
my love for you more fully

I see
the uniqueness that makes you
all you need to be

you are
a part of the collective
broken beauty
of the world

forgiving others
is a wonderfully selfish
act of liberation
even if
no one else knows
you did it

forgive yourself
for what you cannot change
being a little damaged
helps us
to be there for others

I have improved
at not worrying
about what I cannot control

I control so little

which means
I can learn
to worry less

my stress holds no special powers

it is impossible to prove a negative
like
'it never happens'

it probably has happened

negativity
then
from a certain view
is illogical

things happen

Misfortune
finds its power
when we turn it
into Misery

Indeed.

that thing that happened?
it's over
it's okay to stop running

lines in the sand
are meant to be periodically
washed away

fall apart
a little more fully

it is a relief
to stand in a moment
of simplicity

like a tree
standing leafless in winter
letting go
of what is worthless and worn
is how we are reborn

New Moon
tonight I console myself
with infinity

wrap your sadness with a bow
and put it on the shelf

you can take it back
if you ever need it

enjoy
the almost
the before
the not quite

let
the anticipation of renewal
bloom
in your mind

we can listen
to the medicine of others
but ultimately
we must find our own ways
to heal

love is big

love has to be that way
to wrap itself
all the way around us

if you are waiting
for circumstances to shift
so you can be happy
you will never be happy

if you are waiting
to resolve an old hurt
so you can be happy
you will never be happy

if you are waiting
for happiness to find you
so you can be happy
you will never be happy

happiness
is the work of the soul
a simple choice
a difficult choice
the project to carve
an inner oasis
beneath the noise
beneath the surface

the sun shines
on both
the miserable
and
the happy

lift your head
and you can see it

lift your head
as a habit
of feeling tiny rays
of happiness

be open
to the beauty in
the small
the quiet
and
the ordinary

that is where
a good portion of it lives

victimize yourself
and no one else will have to

recognize your strength
and no one else will need to

in your life
it's all up to you

life
will continue to push
until you walk
the path

then
you will find
what has been readying

the truth will keep reminding us of itself

we search
for home
until we discover
that home
originates within us

and then we find it

caterpillars
find their hidden wings
but do not
show the challenge
of their metamorphosis

strength
is not rigid

it is a flexible tree
that survives
rough winds

if out of loss
you keep a giving heart

you have won

when one door closes
another door opens

what they do not tell you is

the door that opens
is often
within yourself

usually so.

you are
only as strong
as you let yourself become

you are
a seed
that pushes through the soil
to unfold
the waiting flower of you

your body
is a work of art
a kinetic sculpture
a memoir written in flesh
the story you reveal
is the journey of your life
an intricate narrative of
perseverance
and
joy

natural and unadorned
I am creating a beauty

aging and exquisite
but it is not a tree

enduring and vibrant
but it is not an ocean

I do not
add it to myself like clothing

or
reflect it as a moon

I am glowing a beauty as I
birth it from within

I am
creating a sun

your body
is a part
of the planet
and
your breath
is a part
of the atmosphere

you
are the interface between
earth
and
sky

if you feel
your heart
is eager to rain
bring it a gift
of sunshine instead
and marvel
at the glorious colors
it makes

if you keep the mountain
in your mind
as you move through the valley
the mountain
will know
where to find you

you can be certain
it is your path
if you
are the one who clears it

all strands are woven
and so
having what you want
means
having what you do not want
along with it

this is what
having what you want
looks like

we strive
for more
but often
the answer
is less

be a cloud

embrace impermanence
and
the balance
between
holding and letting go

blooming holds withering in it

withering holds blooming in it

the long work
of a river

the temporary task
of a cloud

each do
what they need to do

each are
what they need to be

be a healing drop in the water of the world

if you want to find
a problem
you will find one

if you want to see
the goodness
you will see it

I have faith
in what I cannot see

the river runs
even now

when you are unsure
which way to go
each obstacle
is a distraction

choose anyway

every path
needs some clearing

you will leave
the familiar
create
a new place
surrender
but not fully
love
falter and rise
basically
you will survive

if
you want to experience
serenity
you cannot cling
to the cacophony

misfortune
will not become
a part of you
if you do not
weave it
into your bones

strength
knows how to be gentle
when to be patient
and
when to walk away

build from the ruins
more skillfully
this time
from the practice

is your happiness
dependent
on what you have?

I am grateful for what I have not yet completed

do not
squander yourself
or
deplete yourself
completely

refill your well
drink deeply

live to give
another day

do not let them have
all of you

keep something for yourself
a dream
a feeling
a corner of the mind
yours

Hope and Fear sit on a see-saw
and
neither one knows
what will happen
next

act fearlessly
as if dreams are inevitable
and the universe
will believe
you are right

the less fearful I am
of fear
the more courage I have
to be happy

being happy might be the hardest thing you ever do

the river says
it is not enough
to divert from an undesired path
you must also
pave the path you want

move in the right direction
be persistent

flow around obstacles
patiently smooth them
or
find another way

do not so willingly muddy the clear essence of you

the things I know
without looking...
moon shadows

the heart has its own sense of direction

make a certain peace
with stagnation

ask it to tea
and stare patiently at one another

when it is time to get up
both of you
will know

:)

it is not
all at once
each being
has a path
each member
changes the whole
but it is not until
a threshold is reached
that the shift is noticed
a forest
arrives as a seed
working
beneath the soil
laughing
that all we notice
are fleeting flowers

focus on the good

the good things are true too

I can stand in the way
of my serenity
as much as anyone else

there is more good
than bad
in the world

if it were not so
we would no longer be here

everything we need
is replenished
on some level

if it were not so
we would no longer be here

the way
we experience the world
is less
what is understood
and more
what is believed
thankfully
we can control this

do not count
the tragedies

if you must count

count the normalcies
and the blessings

after you have seen enough
go wrong
it becomes easier
to notice what is right

so much is right
everywhere

sunbeams
outnumber raindrops
even on a rainy day

if you cannot see
the cycle
or
the harmony
you are looking
too closely

life equilibrates
not
on the scale of leaves
but on the scale of trees

let the leaves fall
as they will

tend the forest

sure
there are many ways
to die

but
there are more ways
to live

a sky
looking for its moon
only to realize
it had it all along

the way I am sky
the way I am moon

it can feel like
an ending
when really
the elements of it are rearranging
to emerge
in a new shape

like a muscle
it takes practice
so I practice

every time
a wave crashes

I hope I was harder to budge
from whatever inner oasis
I have cultivated

that is the best we can do

I hold nameless things
but must name them
to throw them away

forgive

you can always take back your pain if you need it

you know fullness will find you when you fill yourself

each person
exudes a truth
even before they confess it
to others

each person is a truth

if you have difficulty seeing
kindness
in the world

make your own

each sincere gesture
of love
is everything it needs to be
and so
is perfect

be brave

love the transient
love the imperfect
love the broken

(pretty much anything qualifies)

the people I love
when I open myself
to the possibility of it

you cannot prepare for love

love has its own agenda

take your love into the sunshine
take it into the rain and the snow

love likes to get out and stretch a bit
so teach your love to dance
your love already knows the rhythm
with a little coaxing
your love will learn to sing

do not worry
if love wants to go for a walk
no need to follow it
love knows the way home

let your love take a nap
it's not a sprint, after all
do not think your love is lazy
your love just knows
how far it has to go

my heart is a tree
that withers and renews
it logs its age in secret
as it reaches for the sky

when we stop
pursuing the old dream
and are grateful for what we have

the dream
(perhaps a new dream)

turns around
and finds us

the things that are gone
are gone
so why not
throw them away

what we choose
to hold inside of us
belongs to us
and cannot be taken

people
places
books
dreams
actualities

the moon
slips out of the old light
ready
to put on the new

she knows
how to reinvent herself
in the darkness

it is not
so much what
we endured
but that
we survived

the mind contains
every sunset and moonrise
every heartache and healing
the mind travels farther
than the feet can go

between the clouds
the sky
goes all the way up

once again
I open myself
to the possibility
of the universe

(the universe has quite an imagination)

we are continually
becoming
and
deciding
what we become

do not hold too tightly to a moment

enjoy each one as it arrives
and be open
to the possibility of the next

feel the wetness of running water

the time I thought
the emptiness was empty
and dismissed
the air
that lets me breathe

each of them
wants a part of me
I am Antarctica
belonging to no one
yet bearing many flags

I am
a cratered moon
faded and found
lovely in my shadows
more appealing
than a perfect sphere
for I could never be
that anonymous

it is easy
to love nature

we are nature
and
everything we do
is a part of it

I am falling in love
with the sound
of my breathing

with the feeling of my lungs
as they stretch
and relax

the breath that I borrow
becomes
the boundless sky

the trees and I
marry
in the air

you are
one of the great expressions
of nature
you are
a mountain
a field of wildflowers
a fish
a tree growing toward the sun
a curious wind
beautiful
free

forget luck

you are a revolution
creating the art of you
writing the life of you
speaking the truth of you
becoming and shaping
the being of you

I can see
the river
in the leaves
and the leaves
in the river

the water in a raindrop
is the water in the river

the water of the river
is the water of the body

the molecules of the body
are the memories of a star

where does the substance of the body end
and the substance of everything else begin?

it is like delineating where the sky begins
when the sky

is around us
braided with strands of hair

and within us
feeding blood

it is
a privilege
to provide comfort
and
ease the way
for another
it is
a blessing
to forget ourselves
for a while

let us need each other and be okay with it

the irony
that it takes longer
to find
what is most central
to us

I am the eye of the hurricane

the calm
I am seeking

what I discovered in the darkness
what I discovered in the light

on the road
to renewal

you will leave
the familiar

cross the bridge
or
become the bridge

reach the new place
or
become the new place

you are the season
that is turning

love stretches
and snaps back
perhaps
to a different place
than it was before

there is knowledge
in feelings

you already know
what it is
by the way it feels

dormant buds
on the fingertips of branches
the moment of hope
before I leave
darkness behind

even from the wild fires a new forest comes

the music
of falling apart
rearranged
note by note
in my song of renewal

being strong
is what people do
when they do not have the luxury
of being afraid

cut the tethering ropes
and let the anchors sink

free the tangled strings
and twist them into strong cord

weave a life

if only
happiness were easy
paper flowers
rearranged
in a waterless vase

we learn
to overcome
only the challenges
we face

a mountain
is climbed
by climbing it

happiness
is inside
waiting to be found
it is
the longest journey
to reach the shortest distance

loving
does not require liking
and loving
is more powerful
anyway

you do not need to like
your neighbor
to feel
an inclusive love
for them

tug one string
and the web ripples

the scowl you receive
is the scowl you once gave

so smile
to receive a smile

lessen a burden
and feel your burden lifted

we live together
in the web

and all of us
are tugging on it

each of us
is
as true as a tree
as right as a river

let us name the sunny days
not just the storms

your story
like every story
has happy and sad

tell yourself
the happy
even if it is only
that you survived
the sad

let Sadness rest

there is more to do
than cater to its needs

let yourself
stumble a little

trip yourself open

let the sunlight
warm your soul

we can
seep through the cracks
and find each other

part of us
is liquid
and recognizes our essential commonality

we have a say in
love
home
happiness

they do not happen to us
they arise from us

the actions of others
do not belong to us

we do not need
to own them

be the miracle
in someone's day

an unexpected kindness works fine

kindness
is the only gift

and love
is where it comes from

sit beside the person you do not like

realize all you have in common

if love
were easy to describe
we might be done
by now

love perseveres
because it is unchallengeable

like sunshine
that swallows the shadows

the seed sprouting on a rock
encourages me
to hope
with abandon

I memorize one experience
then another

I gather experiences
as if gathering a field of daisies

my arms
overflowing

I leave a trail
of petals
back to the source

someday *soon*
untethered
I will surely rise
to slip between
the light of the stars

the will
to be happy
is a boat
to put in stormy waters

plug the holes you can
and keep
bailing

if it sinks
build another

a small change
in rudder
affects both the journey
and the destination

a mountain
becomes smaller
the longer it is climbed

by the time
the summit is reached
all that remains
is a valley

you are the journey
that leads back to yourself

you will spend your life
getting there

no one else
will reach

your particular destination

tiny
pleasures
are the hardest ones to lose

nature
leaves its treasures
scattered in plain view
it takes
a careful observer
to see
what is everywhere

nature never asks
how do I look?
or apologizes for its seasons
not even the ones that
dull the colors
burn the plains
send animals to sleep for months
nature
is not flustered when it is ignored
nature knows
what it needs to do
it keeps changing tides
shifting beaches
spinning planets
breathing forests
folding mountains
erupting sidewalks with blooming weeds

we are
interwoven

if you water a seedling
part of you
will bloom

all being made
of the same stuff

she grew her tree tall
she shone her sun brightly
she rode her river
to a new day

this time
in the full of the moon
I will learn to love
its waning too

trust
the journey

the journey has its own wisdom

how long
did it take you to become
who you are today?

your entire life
labyrinthine path and all

how long will it take
to become your future self?

long enough to realize
you already are that person

if we envision
who we want to be
as a light
rather than
a path

then when we
lose the path

the light
of who we want to be
will set us back on course

beauty
is a type of air

overlooked
but sustaining
those who partake
in the
breathing of it

find beauty in each day
a small beauty works fine

bask in it
then let it go

other beauty awaits you

the day stretches long
like paper
the night
folds into itself
hills and valleys
an origami
that finds shape
in the dawn

trees
want you to climb them

rivers
long to delight your toes

hills
stretch for you

the ocean calls for you
in waves

plant a seed
read to a child
feed an animal
write a book
speak from the heart
demonstrate hope for the future

it takes more courage to finish
than to start something new

finishing means letting go

be ready to start again
like the moon

in other breaking news
a silver moon
sailed
above the world
and the only ones
who knew it
were the ones who looked up

fragments
of an overactive mind
carefully written
on scraps of paper…
then released in the wind

ABOUT THE AUTHOR

Kat Lehmann is the author of *Moon Full of Moons* (Peaceful Daily, 2015), which follows a personal transformation from sadness through acceptance and healing to a new happiness. *Moon Full of Moons* is the Winner of the 2016 Royal Dragonfly Book Award.

More than a hundred of her poems have been published in literary journals and anthologies, including the *Connecticut River Review*, *American Tanka*, *Chrysanthemum*, and *Modern Haiku*. She holds a Ph.D. in biochemistry and has worked in research science and research ethics. Her website is www.SongsOfKat.com, and she writes on Twitter and Instagram as @SongsOfKat.

Kat is the proud mother of two children and a companion to her husband, three cats, fifty orchids, and a river. She lives in New England.

ABOUT THE ARTIST

Subhashini Chandramani is an artist who designs, paints, creates portraits, and writes poetry. Her poetry book, *From the Anklets of a Homemaker*, was published in 2013. Her "Garden Art" has touched hearts across India and the world, evidenced from her popularity on multiple social media channels and coverage of her art in newspapers, websites and magazines. Her work has been quoted in *Buzzfeed, Metro UK, The Hindu, She the People, Huffington Post*, and many regional newspapers and magazines. When she is not playing with art she is gardening and listening to music.

Subhashini has an online gallery at https://neelavanam.in/ where Garden Art lovers can get their own copy of their favourite Garden Art. You can follow her work on Instagram and Twitter at @neelavanam.

Subhashini can be contacted at subhashini.chandramani@gmail.com

Beyond the landscaping of our first home was a dense thicket I liked to explore. Walking through the thicket was slow work, and my path was often determined by the wild brush, scrambling shrubs, and young trees. Oh! There were trees that were overcome with clinging vines and tall grass such that I did not notice them until I trampled into the thicket. Whenever I discovered a tree, I would carefully liberate it from the plants that were swallowing it whole. I continued to work in this way, hours at a time, until I trudged back to the house exhausted, dirty, and thorn-scratched. When I closed my eyes, images of the multiflora rose monoliths would persist. When I slept, vines would infiltrate my dreams. I rescued 29 trees that summer – trees I did not know needed to be freed until I ventured into the dense thicket, trees I didn't know I could save until I saved them. As we walk deeper into our inner wild places, may we discover the beautiful trees, perhaps covered in vines, that await us. Trees that we can save.

Facebook: 29Trees
29Trees@sbcglobal.net

Dear Reader,

I hope you continue to enjoy *Small Stones from the River*. I have been writing and collecting these "small stones" for years, and I am thrilled to share some of them for you.

Small stones are tiny awarenesses of the inner and outer world that find their form somewhere between mindfulness meditation and poetry writing. I wrote many of them while sitting beside my favorite river. The author photo of my book *Moon Full of Moons* shows me sitting on a large river stone that helped me notice the smaller stones.

As an author, I appreciate reader feedback and hearing what you liked, what you loved, and even what you didn't like. Feel free to connect with me at the places below.

Reviews can be elusive these days. You, the reader, can have a tremendous impact on the book by letting potential readers know what you thought about it. Please consider posting a simple review on Amazon or GoodReads.

Thanks for reading *Small Stones from the River* and meditating with me.

With gratitude,
Kat Lehmann

Website: www.SongsOfKat.com
Facebook: @SongsOfKat
Twitter: @SongsOfKat
Instagram: @SongsOfKat

SMALL STONES TO PUT IN MY POCKET:

44083179R00119

Made in the USA
Lexington, KY
06 July 2019